Ink on paper

underground
coloring
book

by Kyo Smith

Kyo Smith

Ink on paper

Introduction

If you are one of the lucky few to have a copy of this coloring book in your hands... prepare yourself. You have been personally invited to delve into the mind of an underground artist, if but for a few moments of your time.

The pages lying within, are but a small selection of the many images I have created over the years. These images would not be, if not for my struggles, dreams, nightmares, and the harsh reality of urban life.

I have created this book not only to showcase some of my artwork, but to inspire the artist within us all.

Thank you for all of your support!

-Kyo Smith

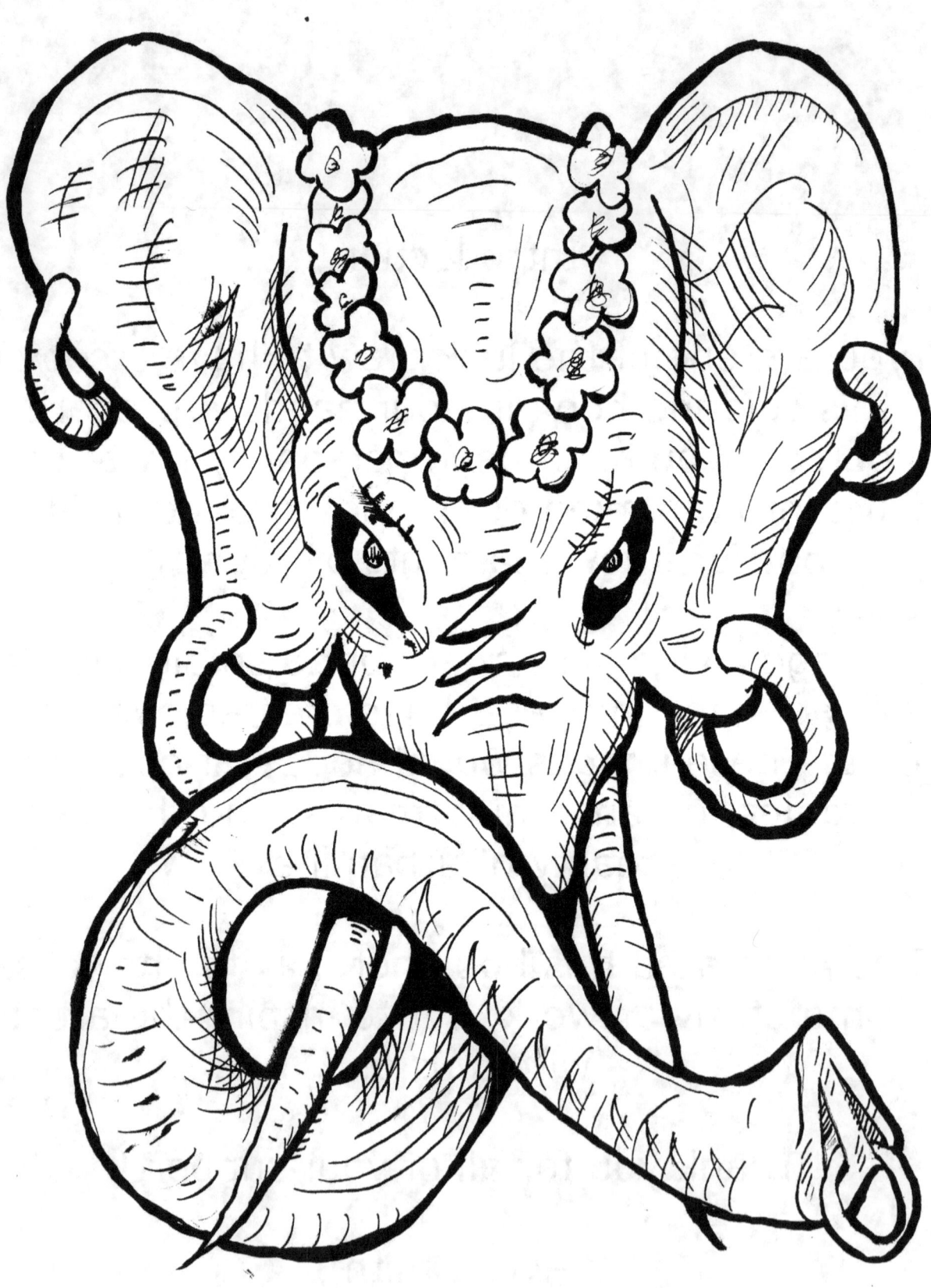

Ink on paper

Ink on paper

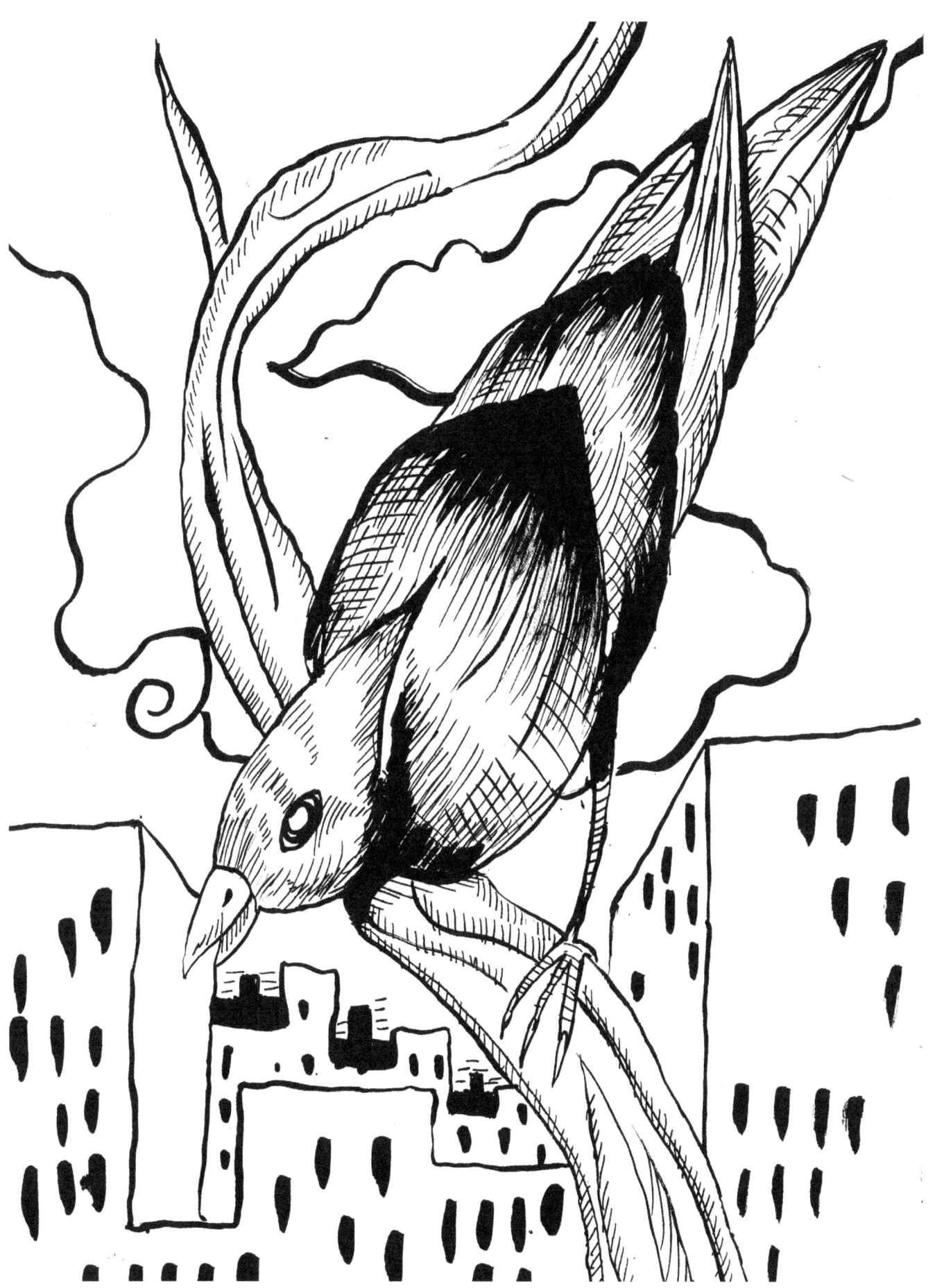

underground coloring book

Kyo Smith

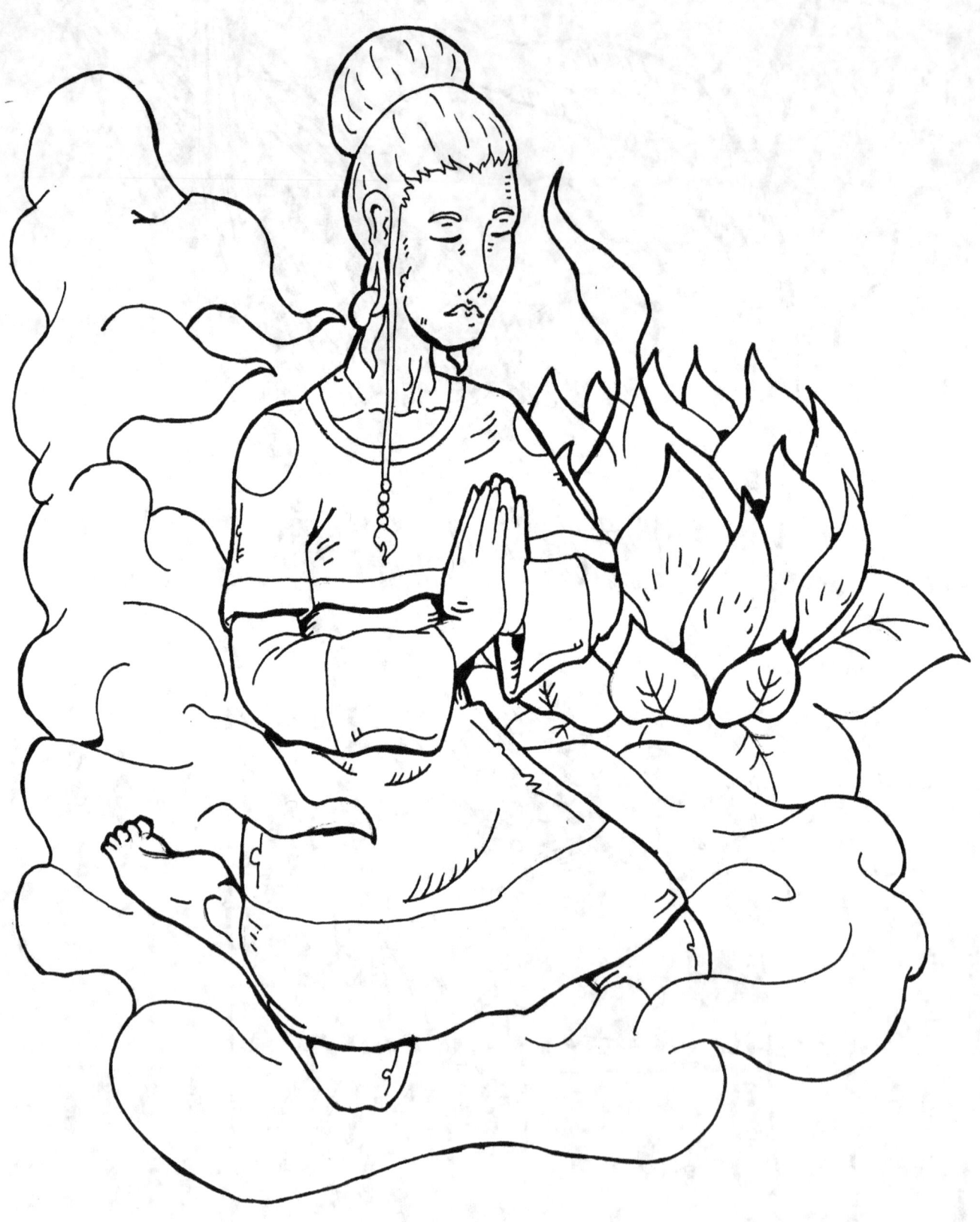

Ink on paper

Ink on paper

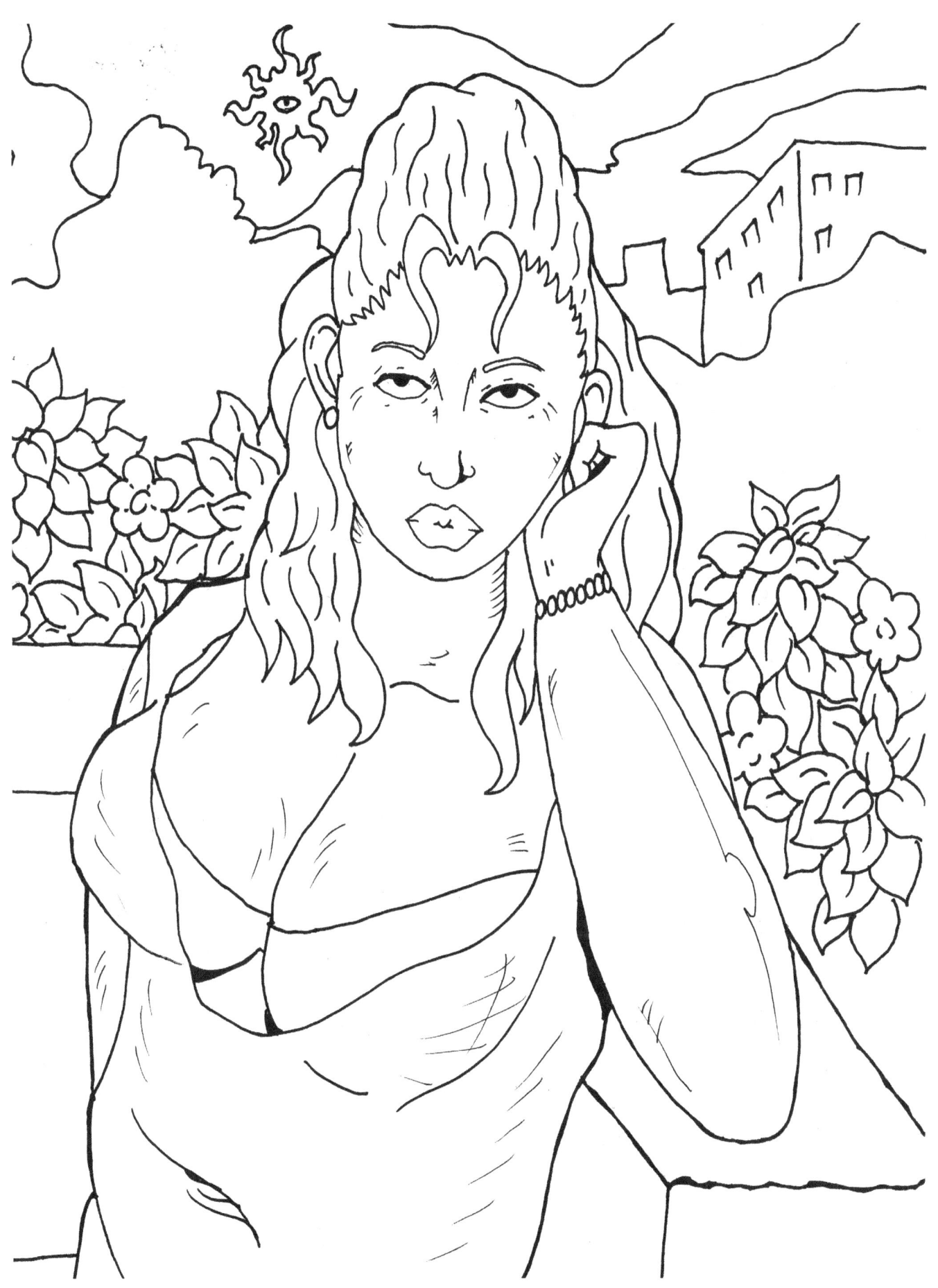

underground coloring book

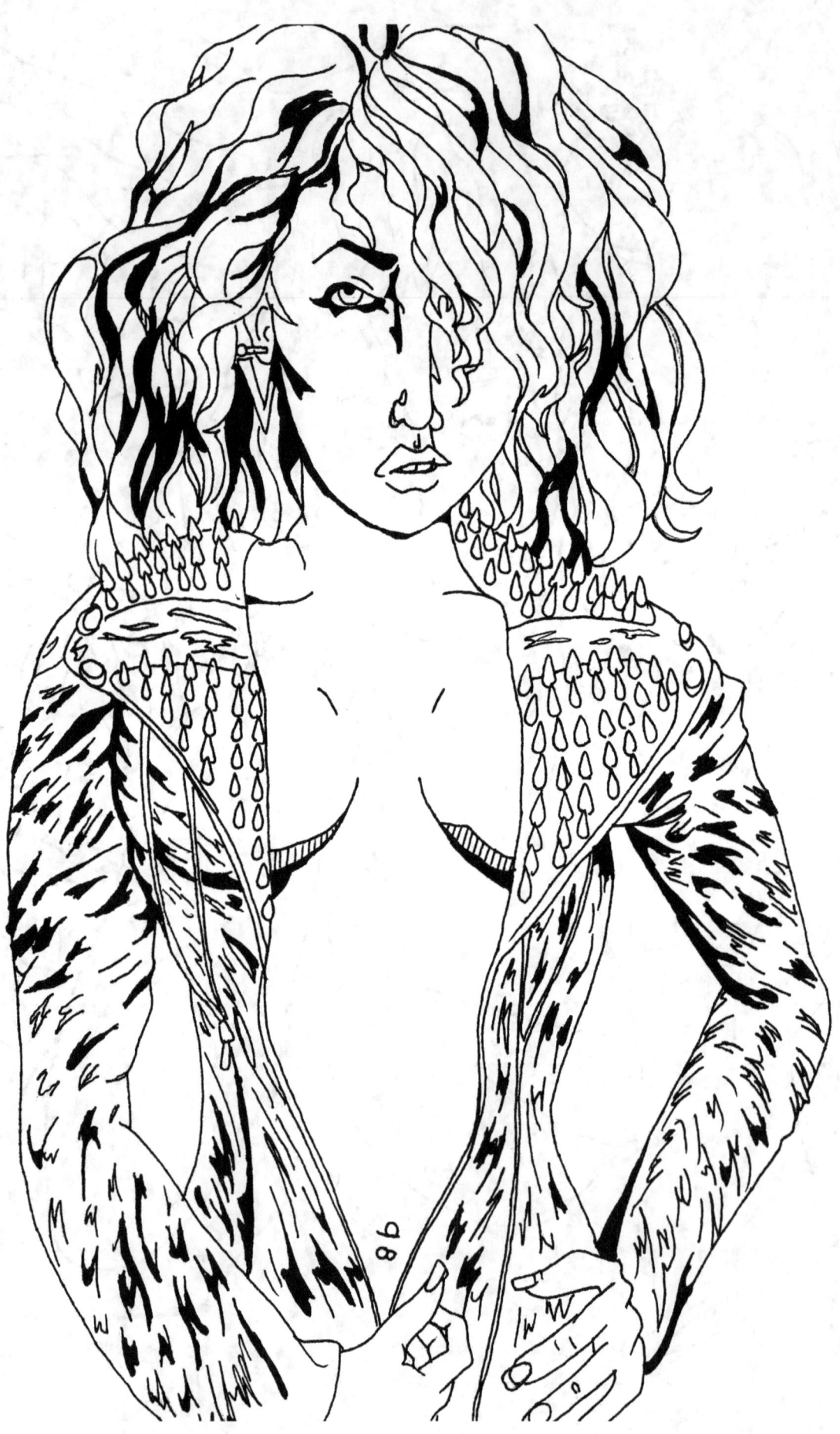

Ink on paper

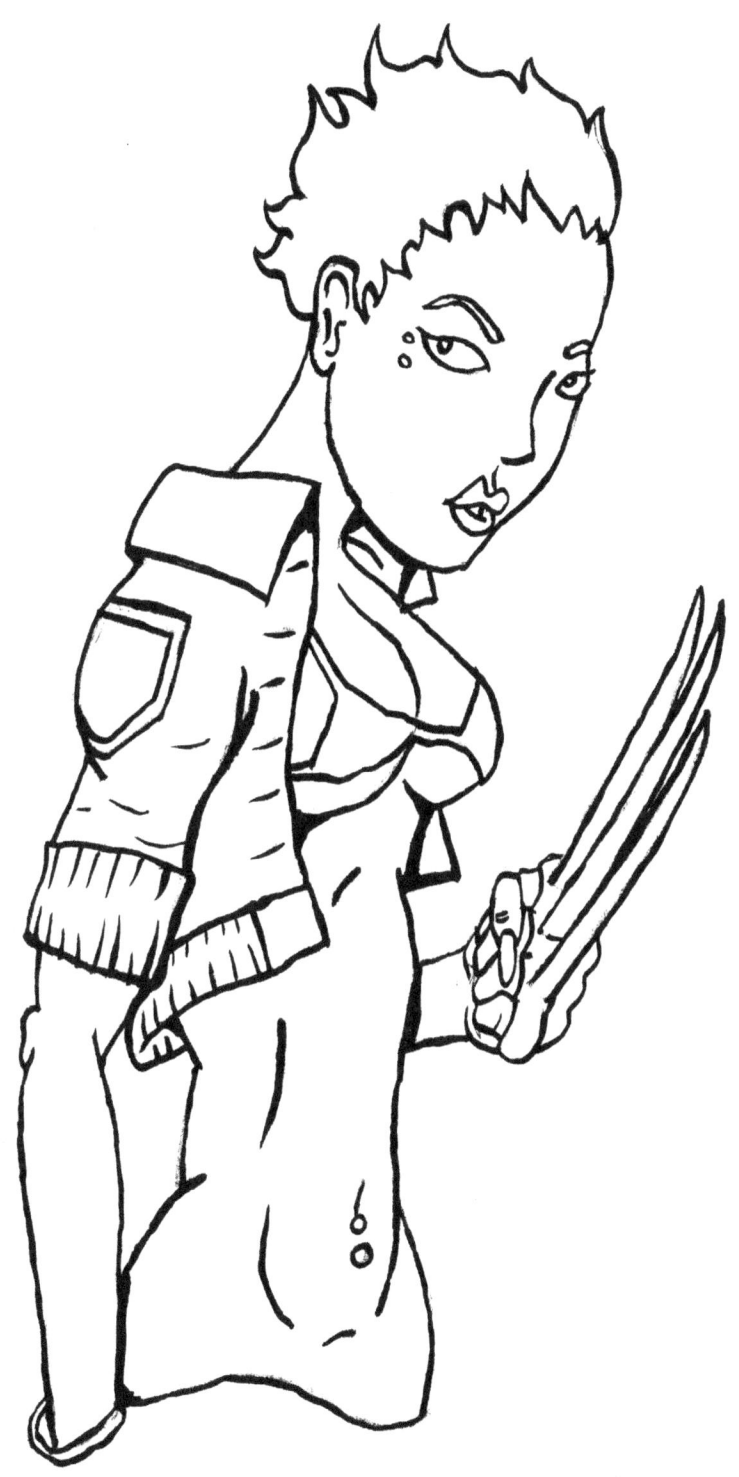

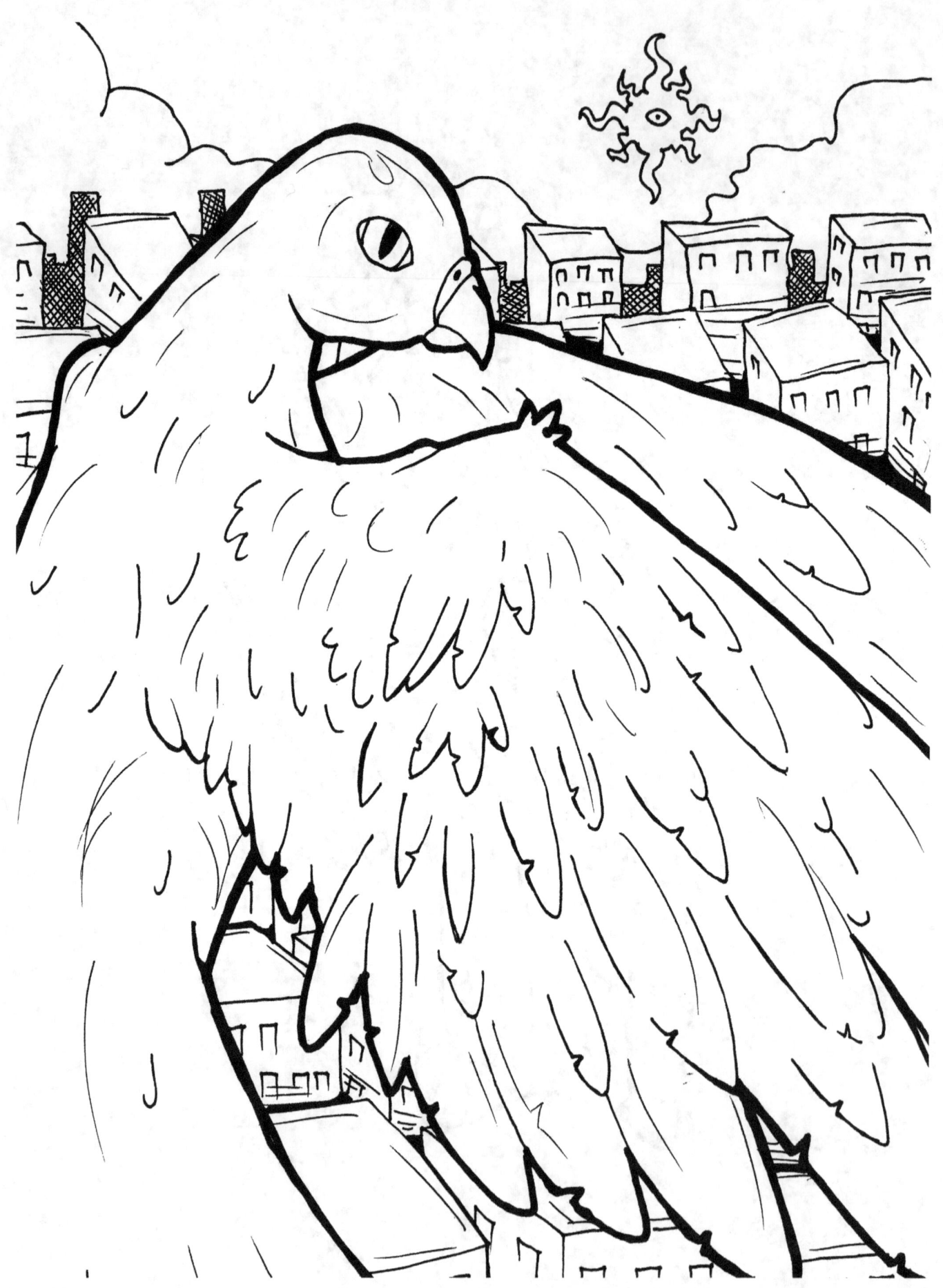

Ink on paper

Ink on paper

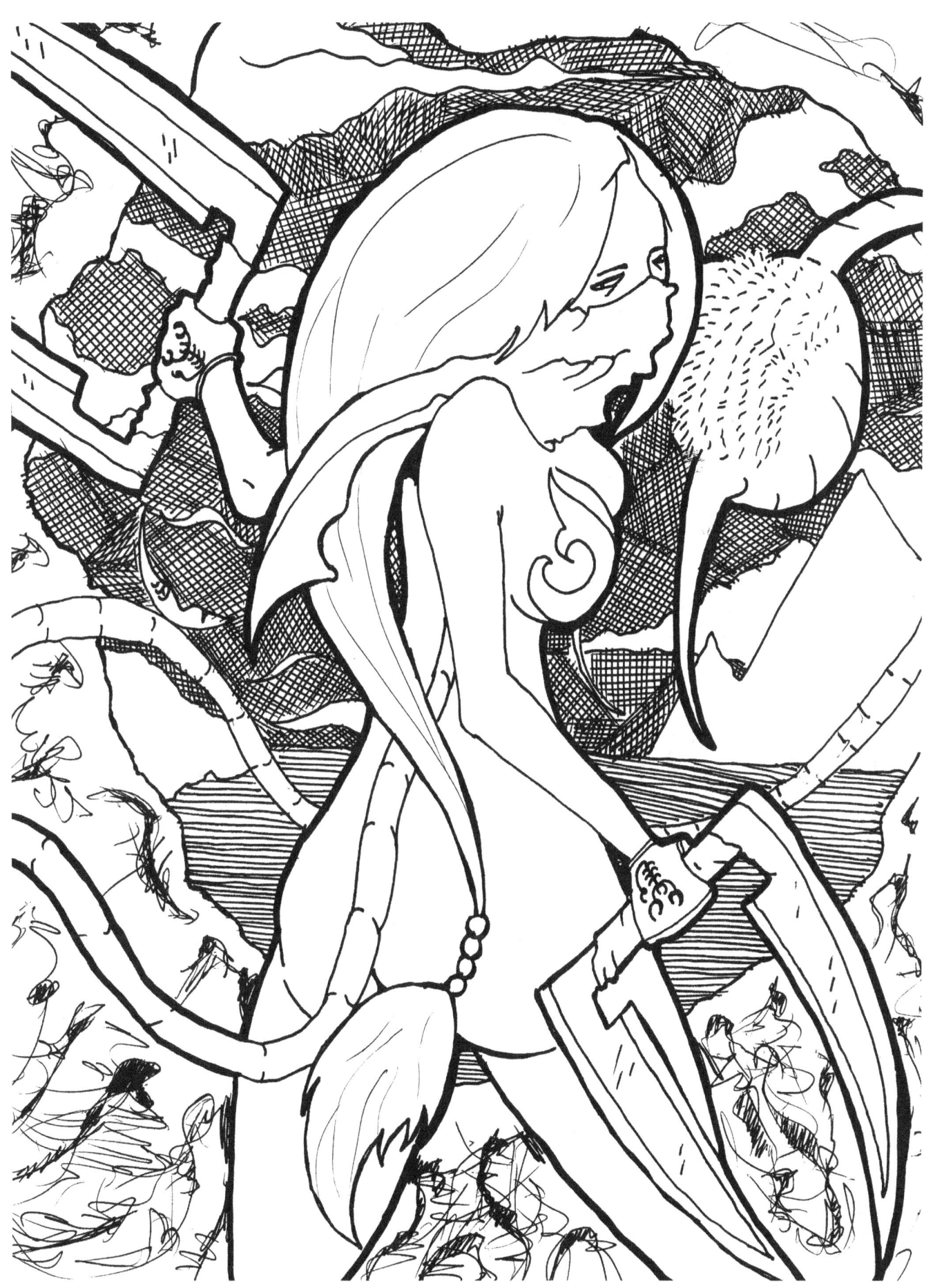

underground coloring book

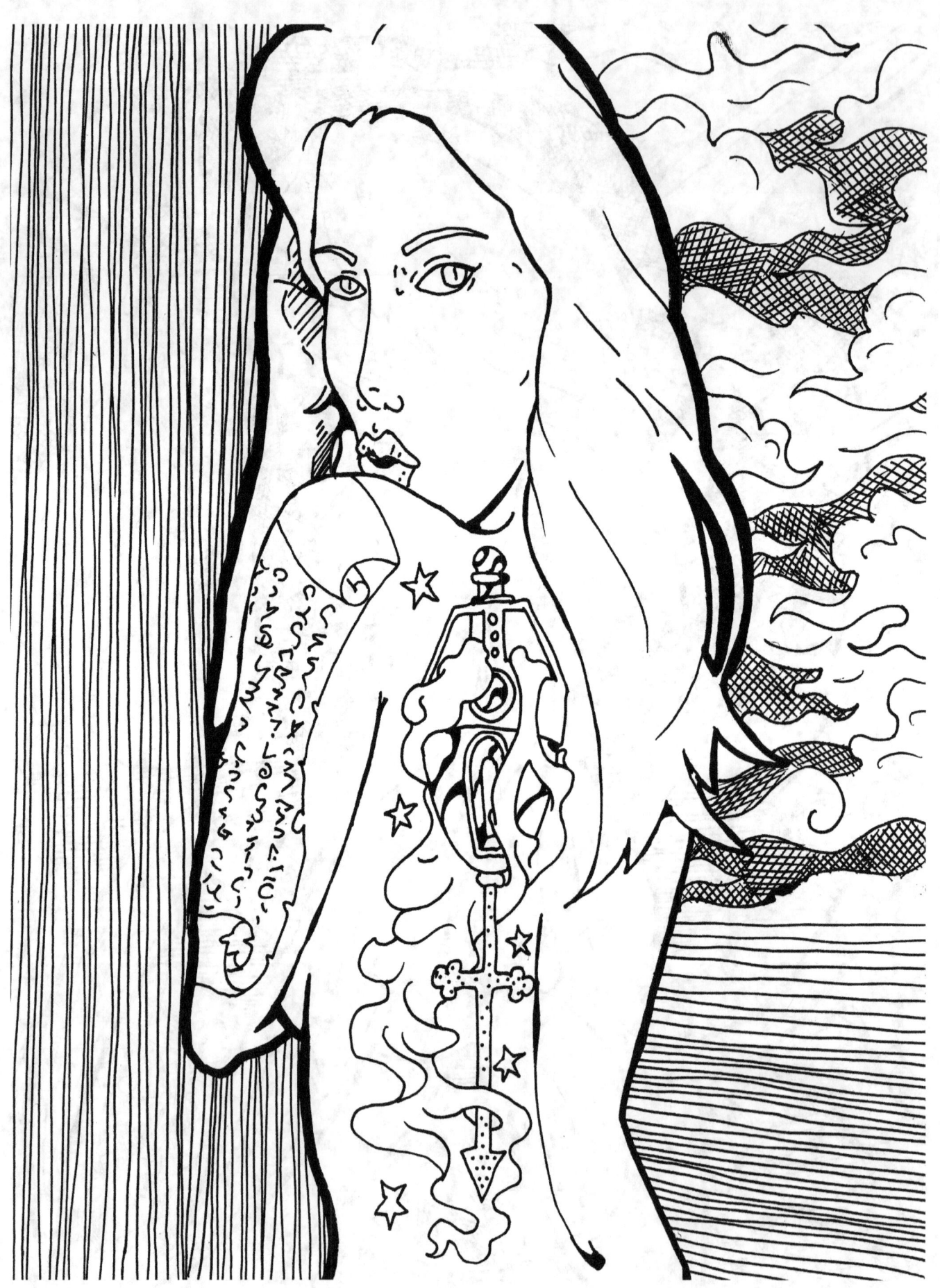

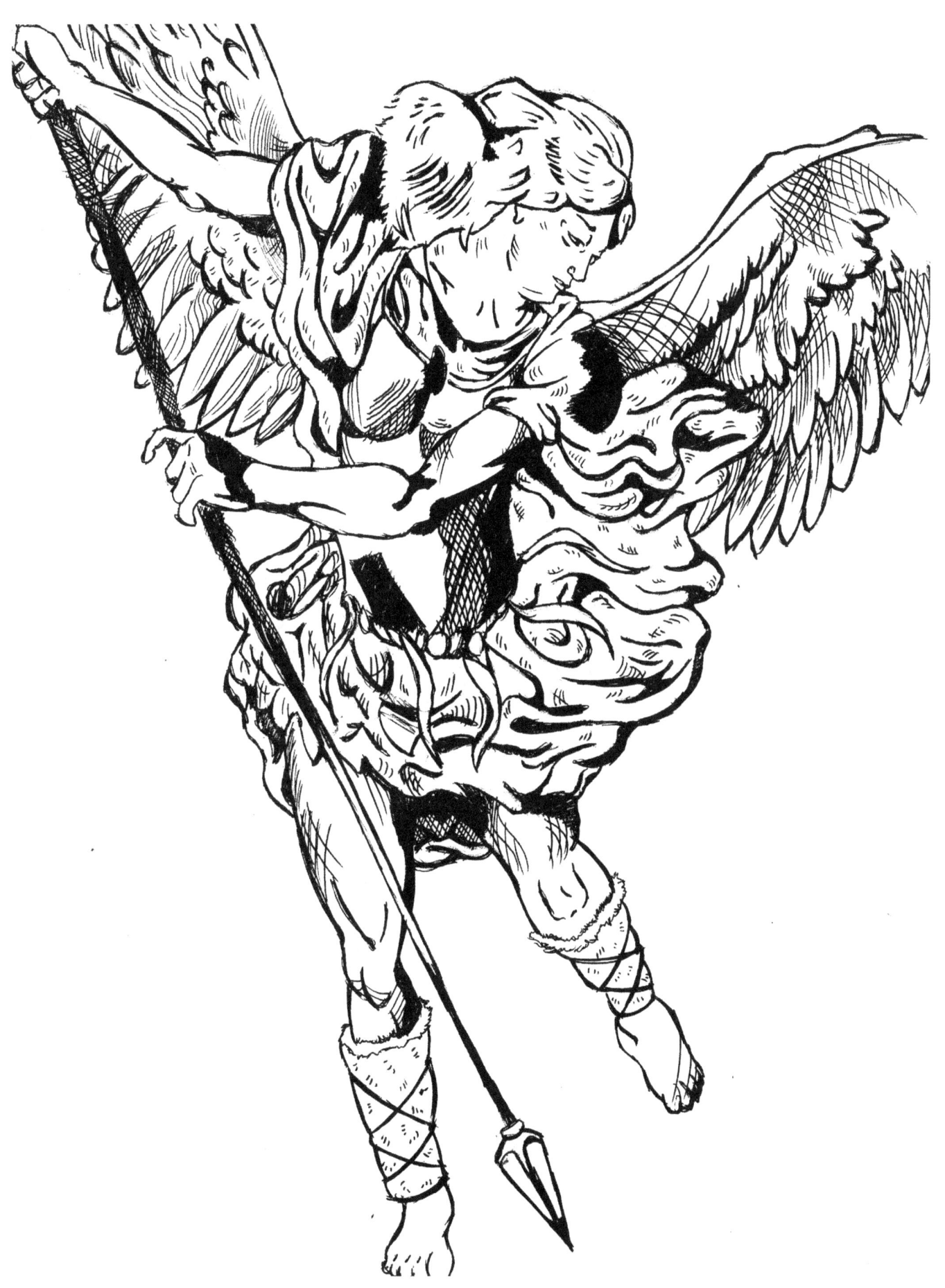

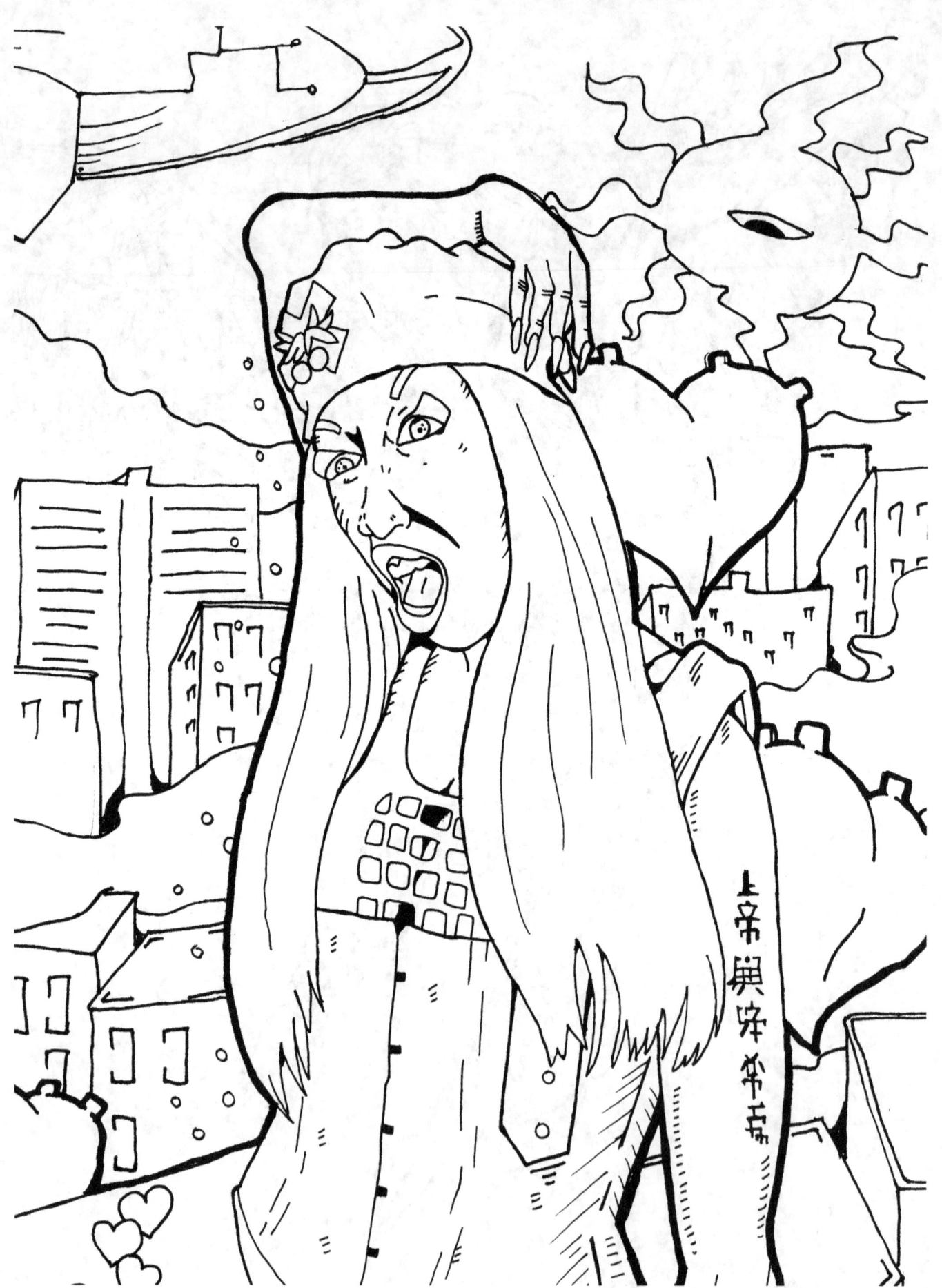

Ink on paper

Ink on paper

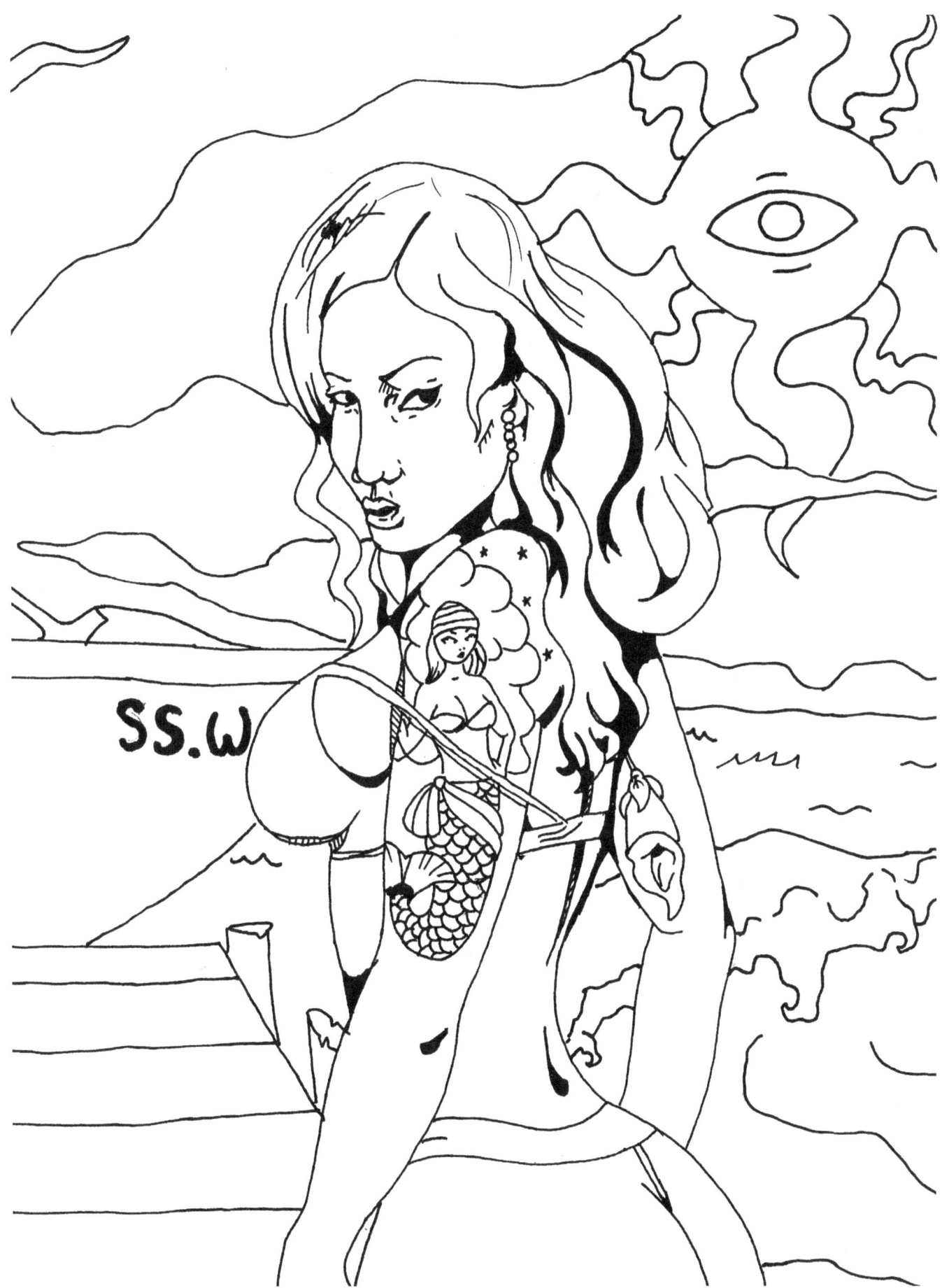

underground coloring book

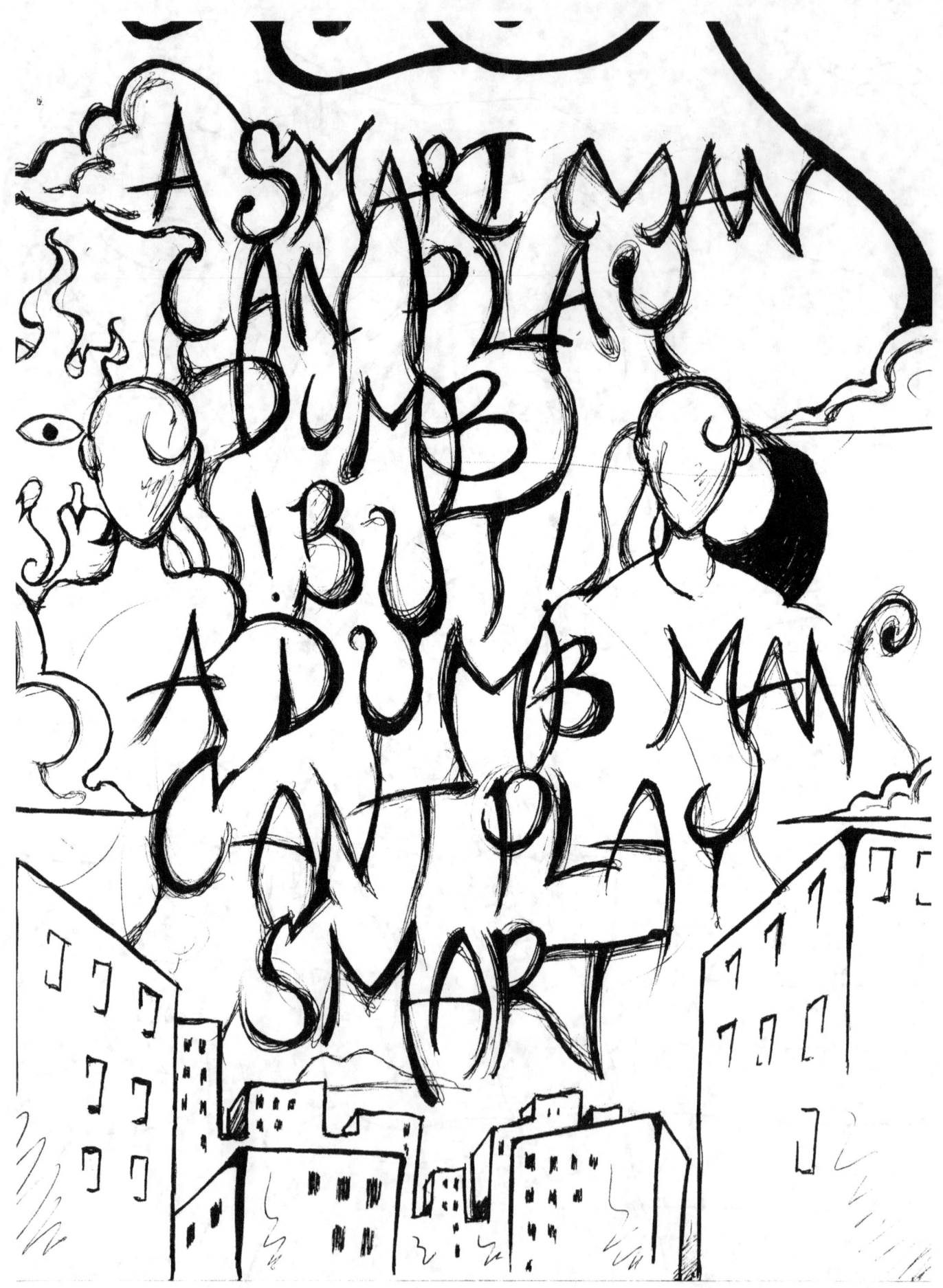

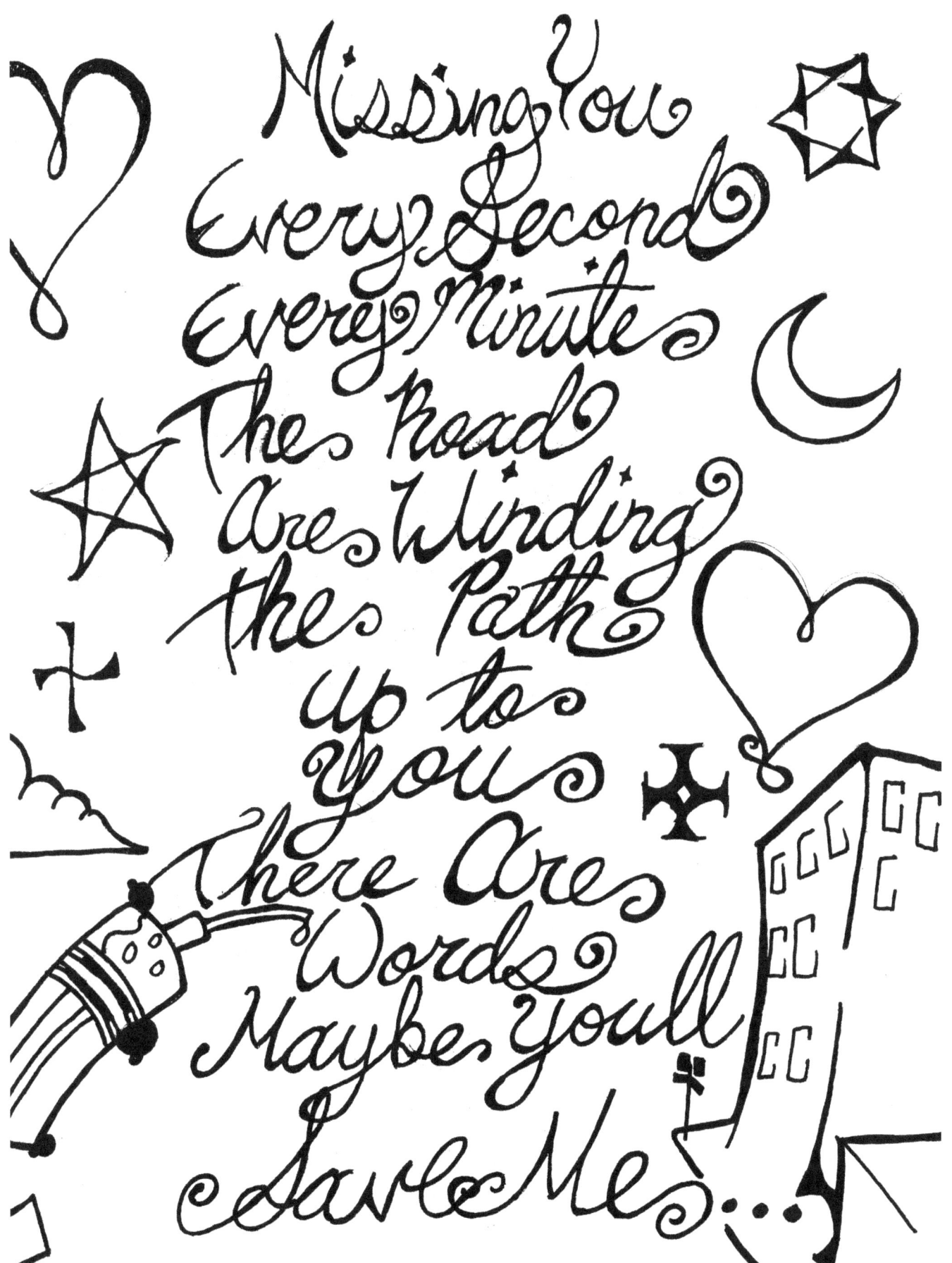

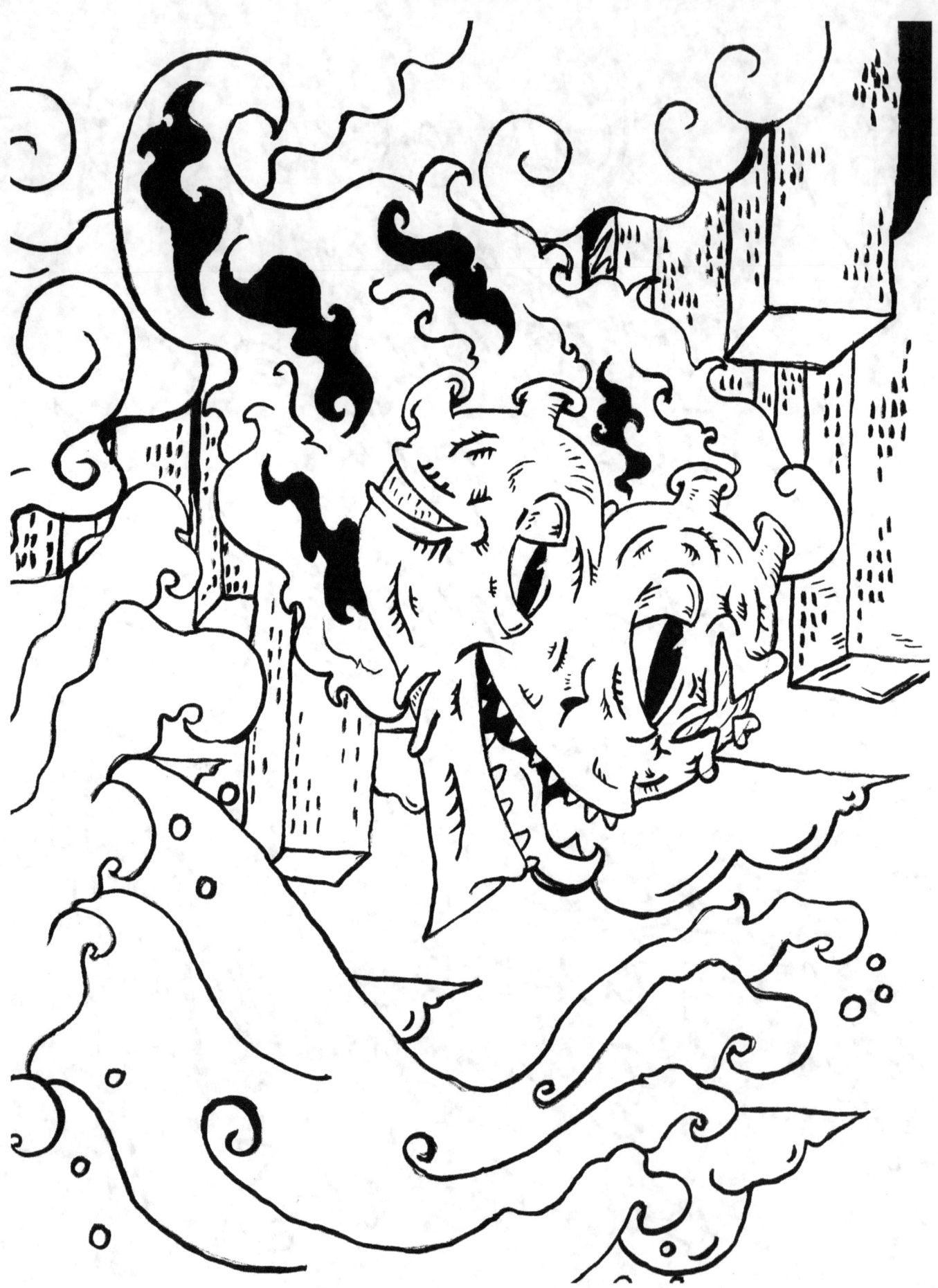

Ink on paper

Ink on paper

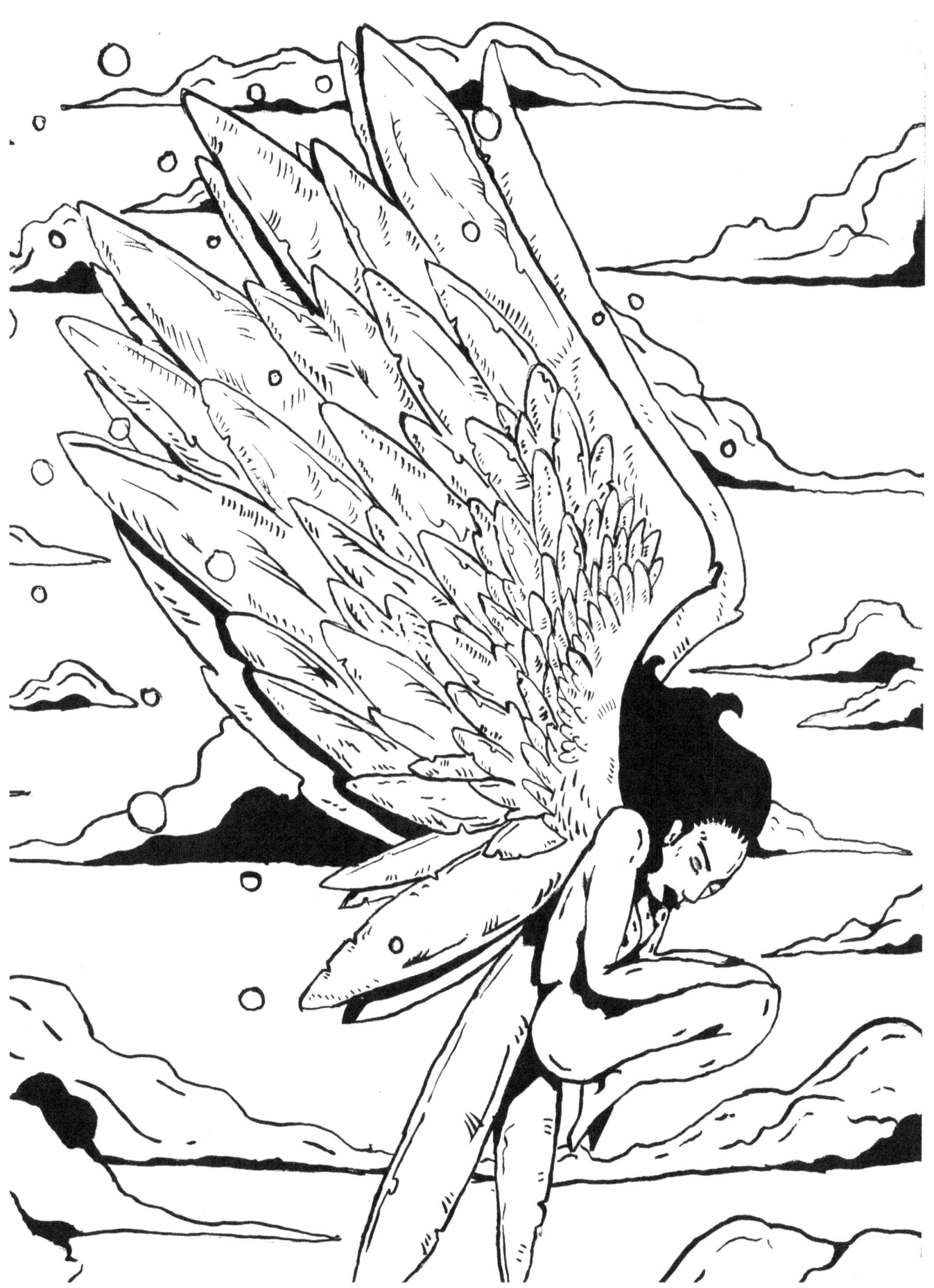

underground coloring book

Kyo Smith

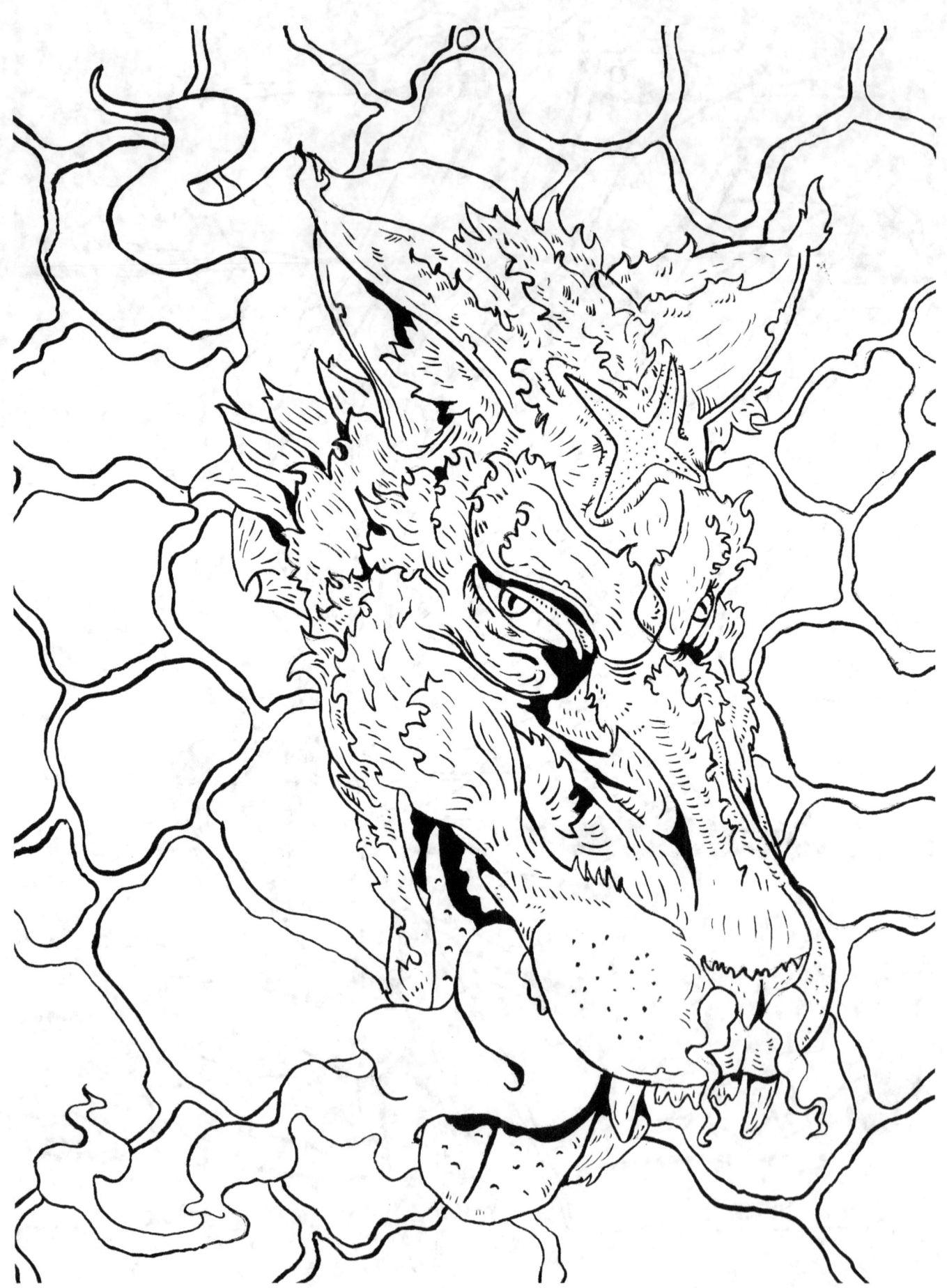

Ink on paper

Ink on paper

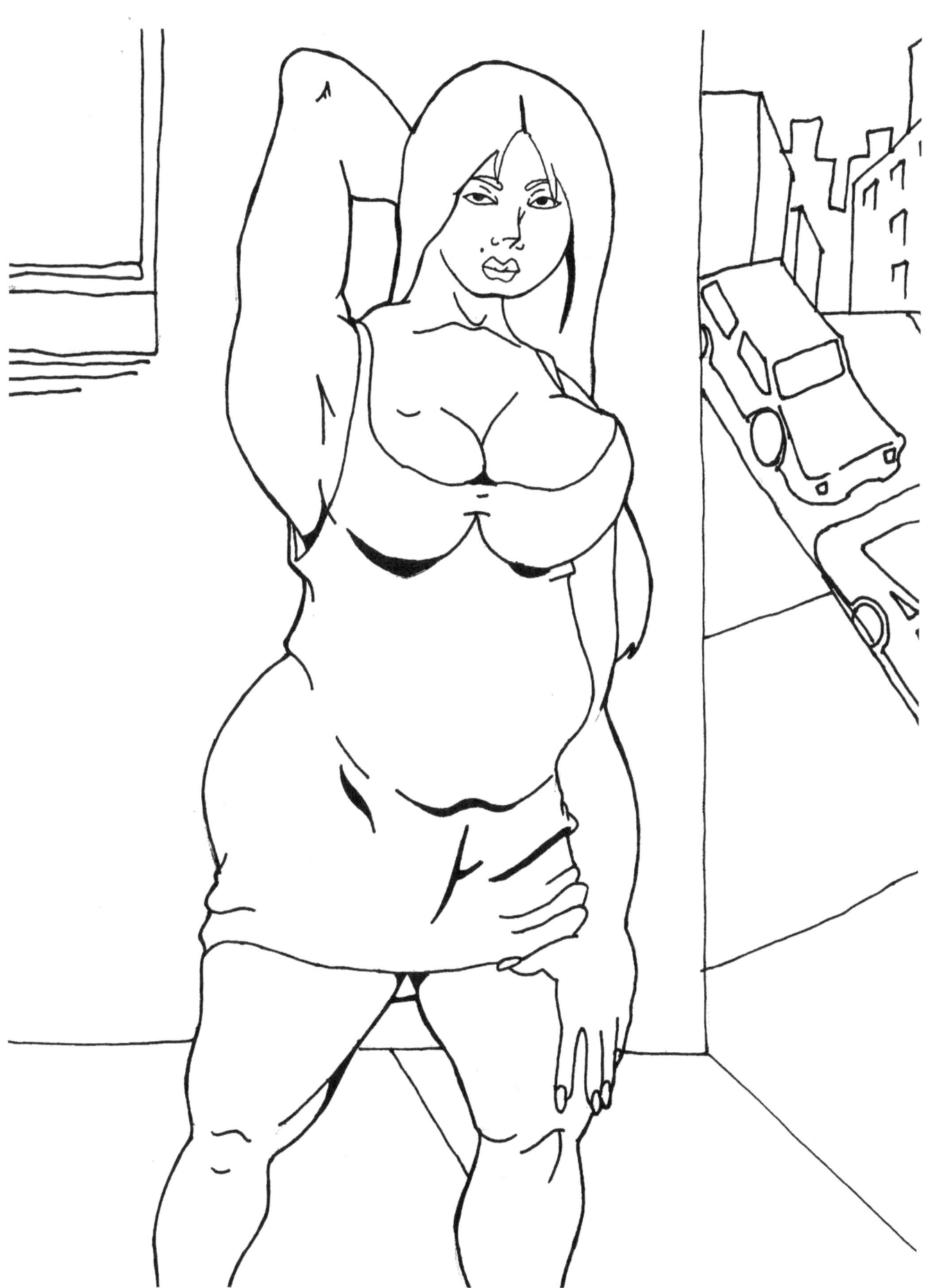

underground coloring book

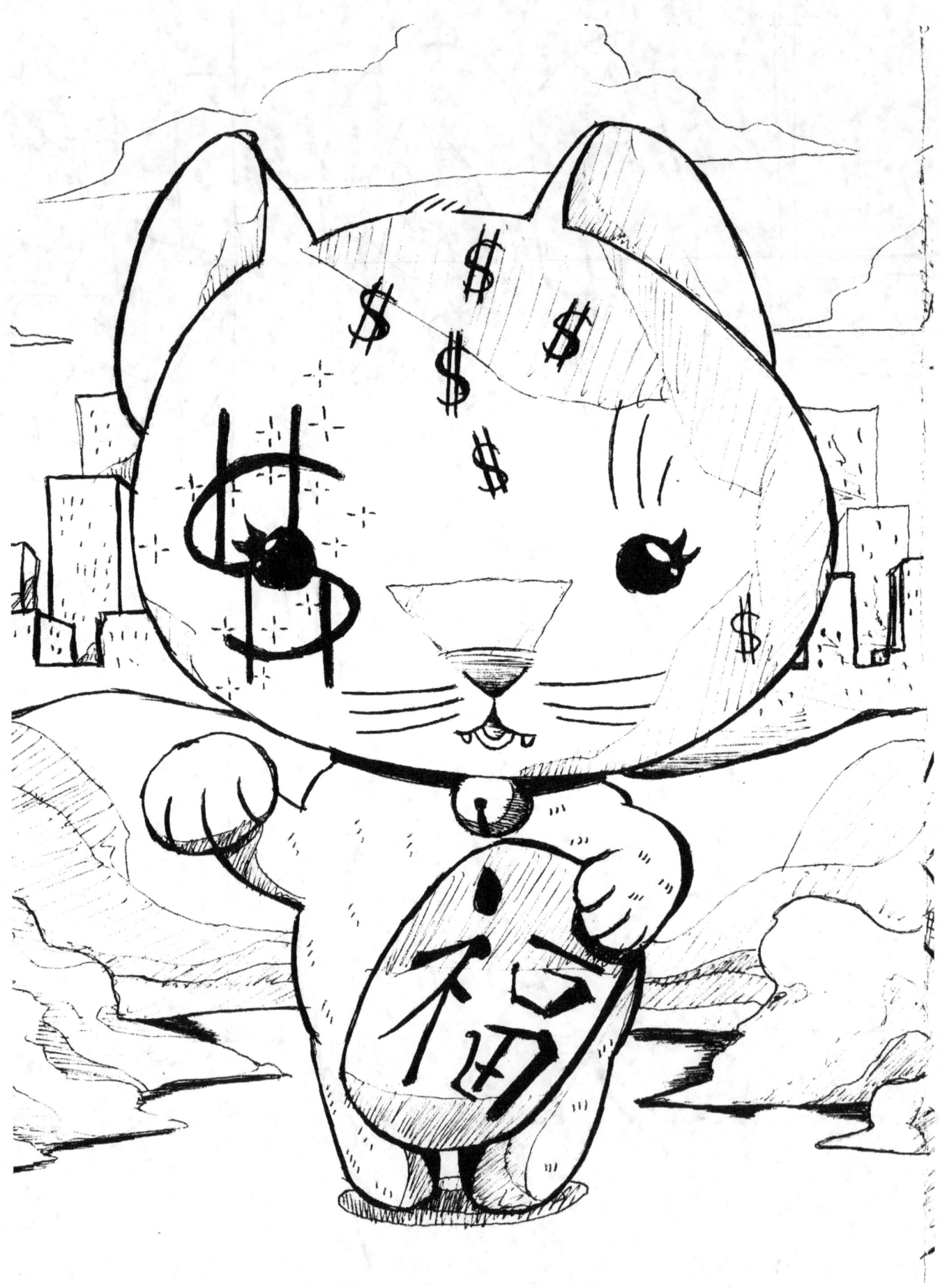

Ink on paper

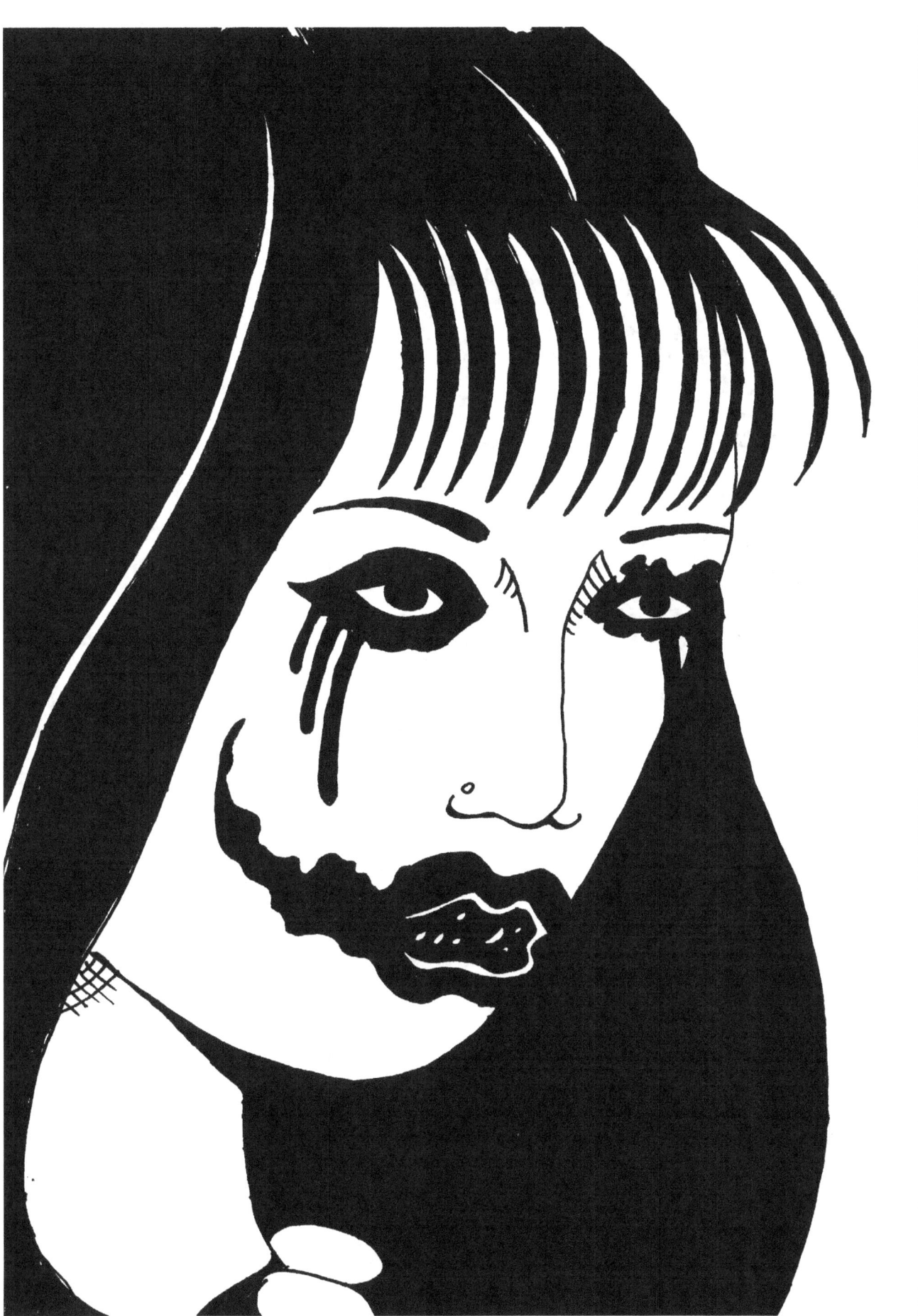

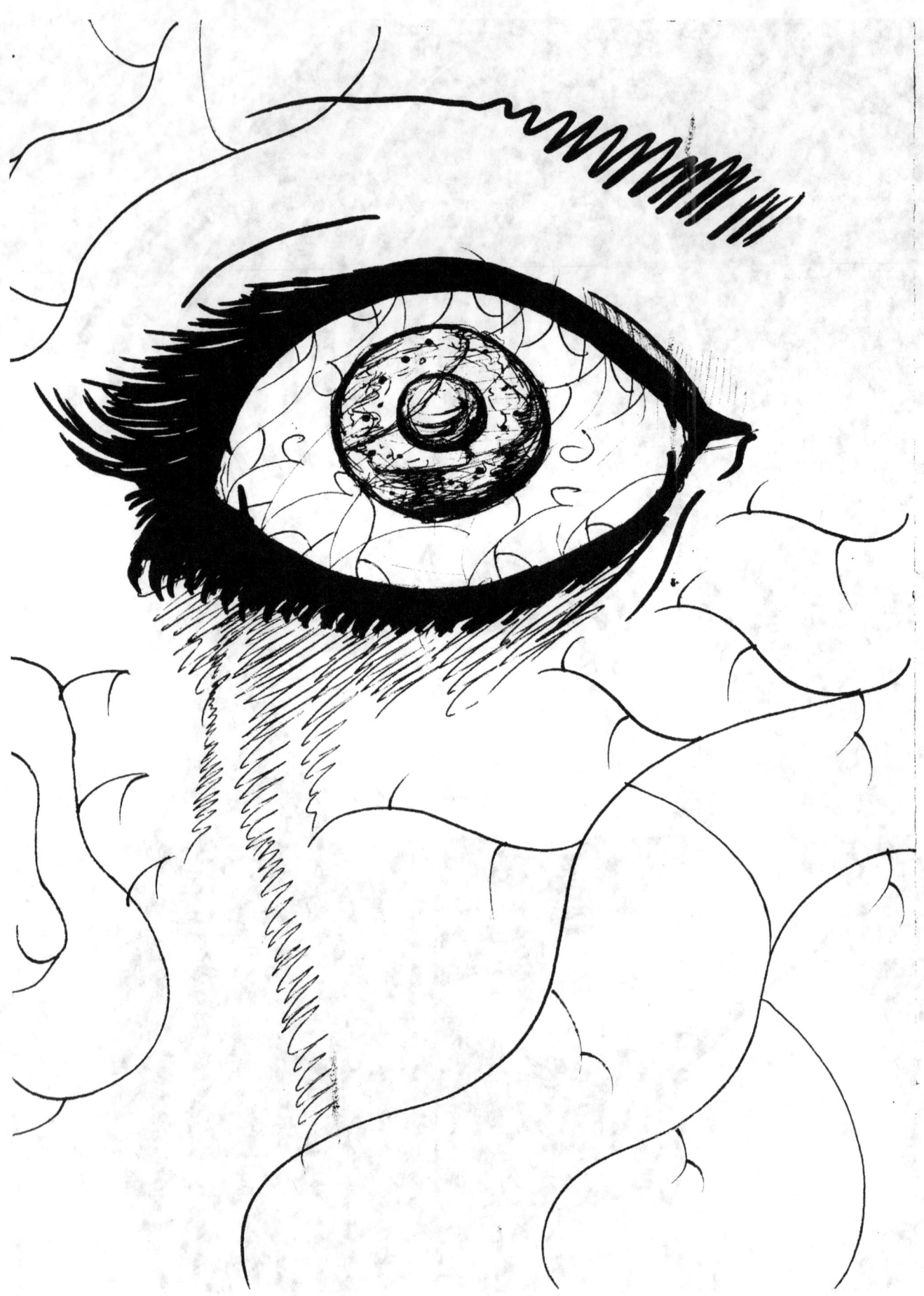

Ink on paper

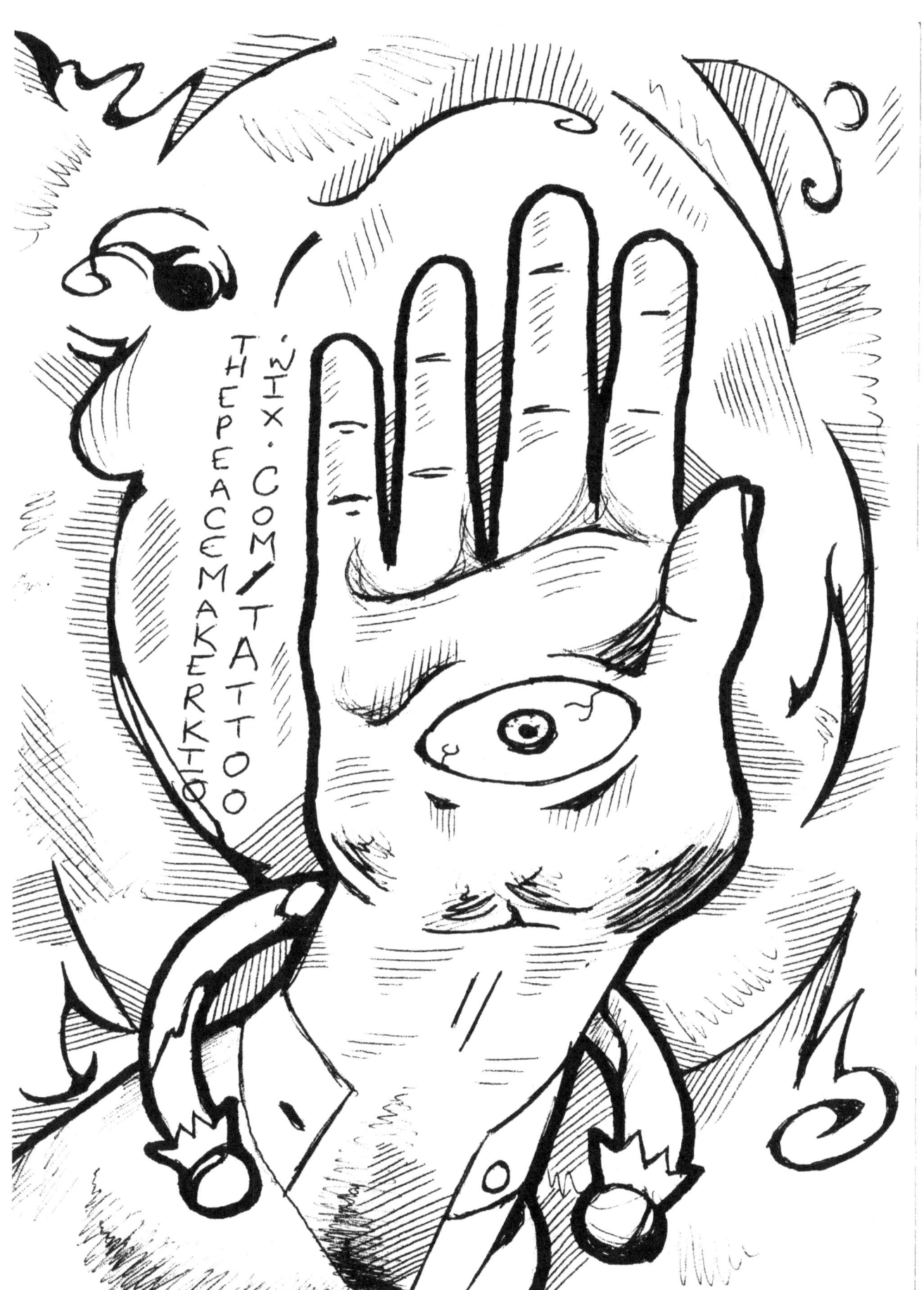

THEPEACEMAKERKTO.WIX.COM/TATTOO

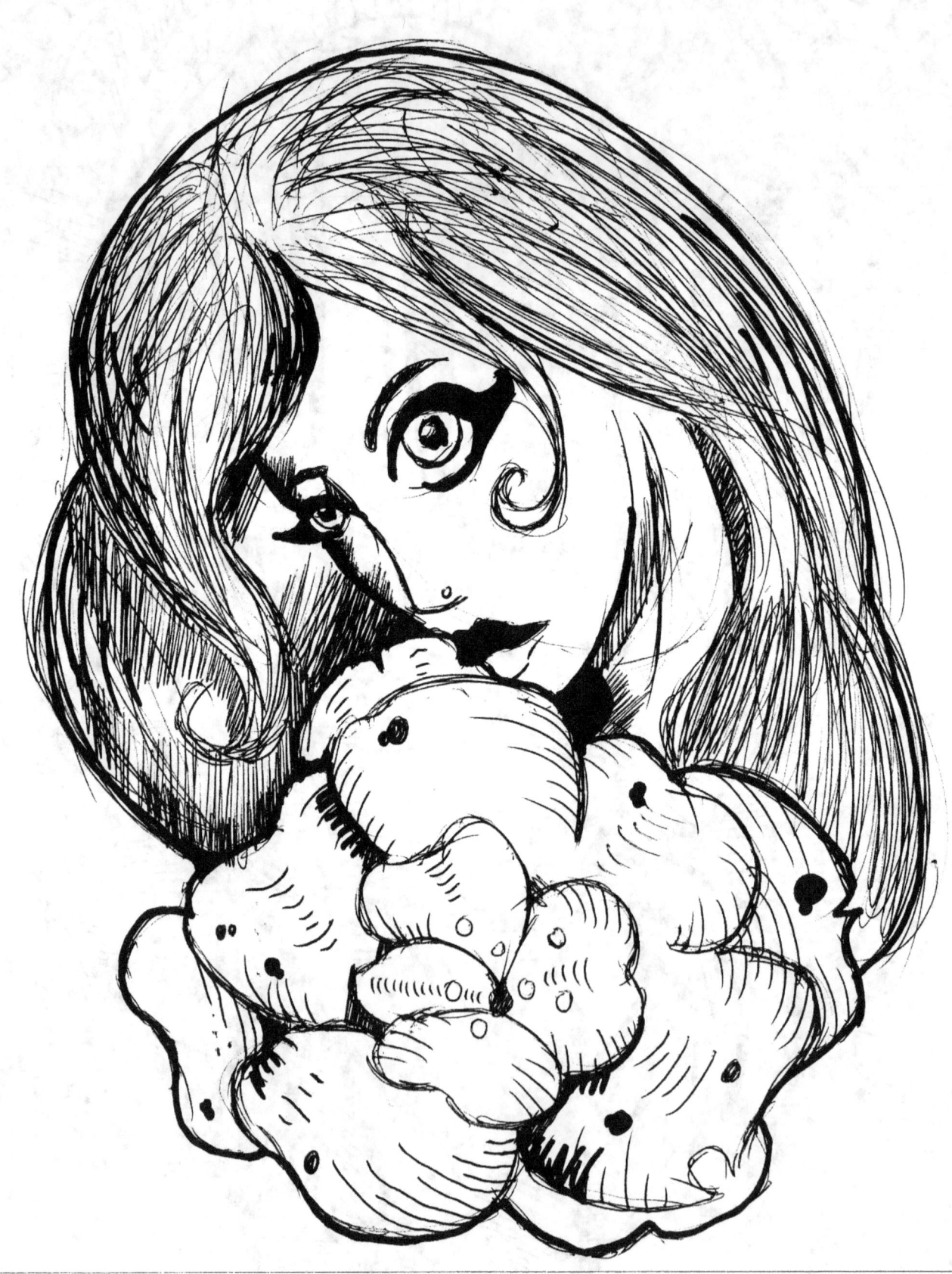

Ink on paper

Ink on paper

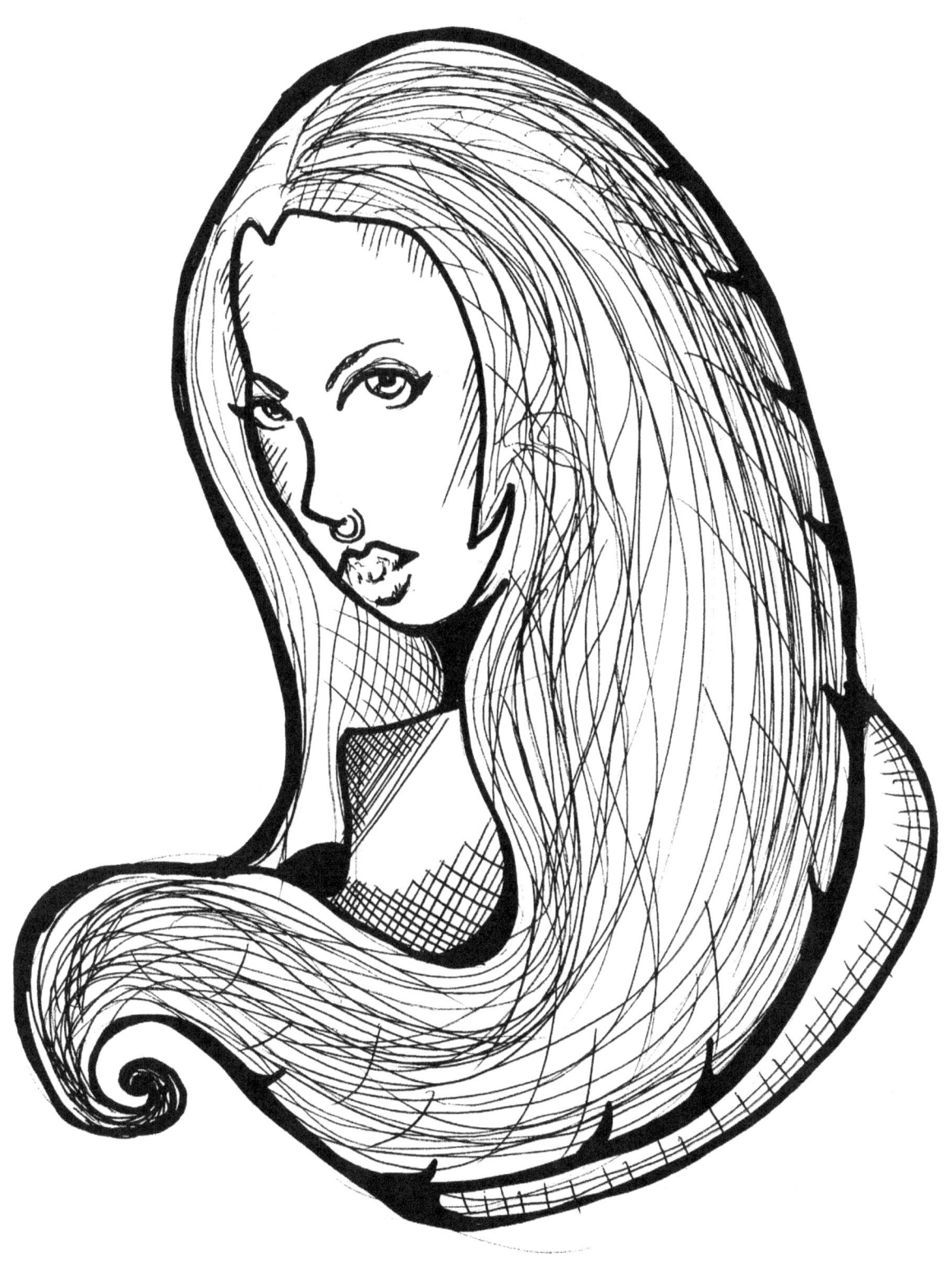

Kyo Smith

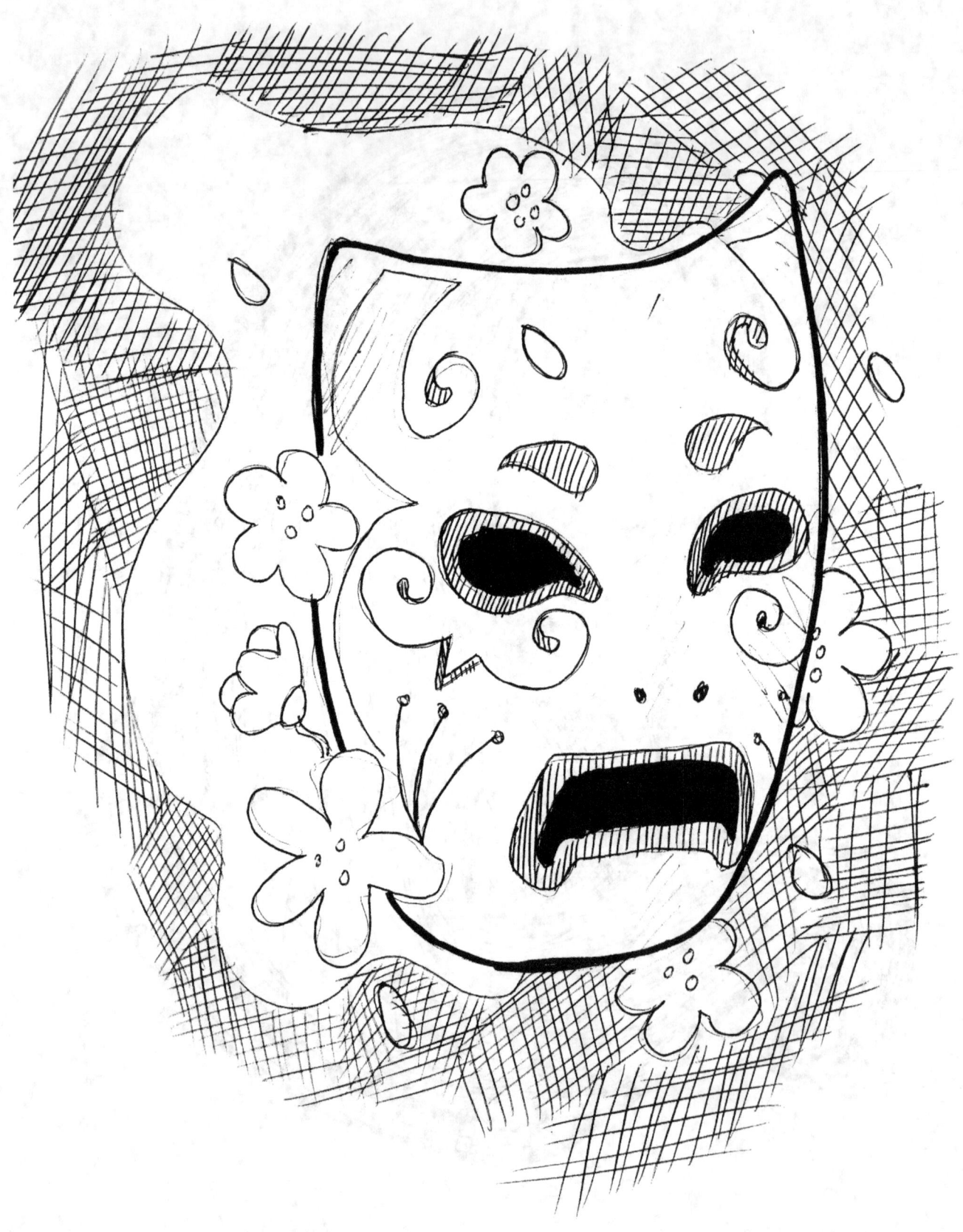

Ink on paper

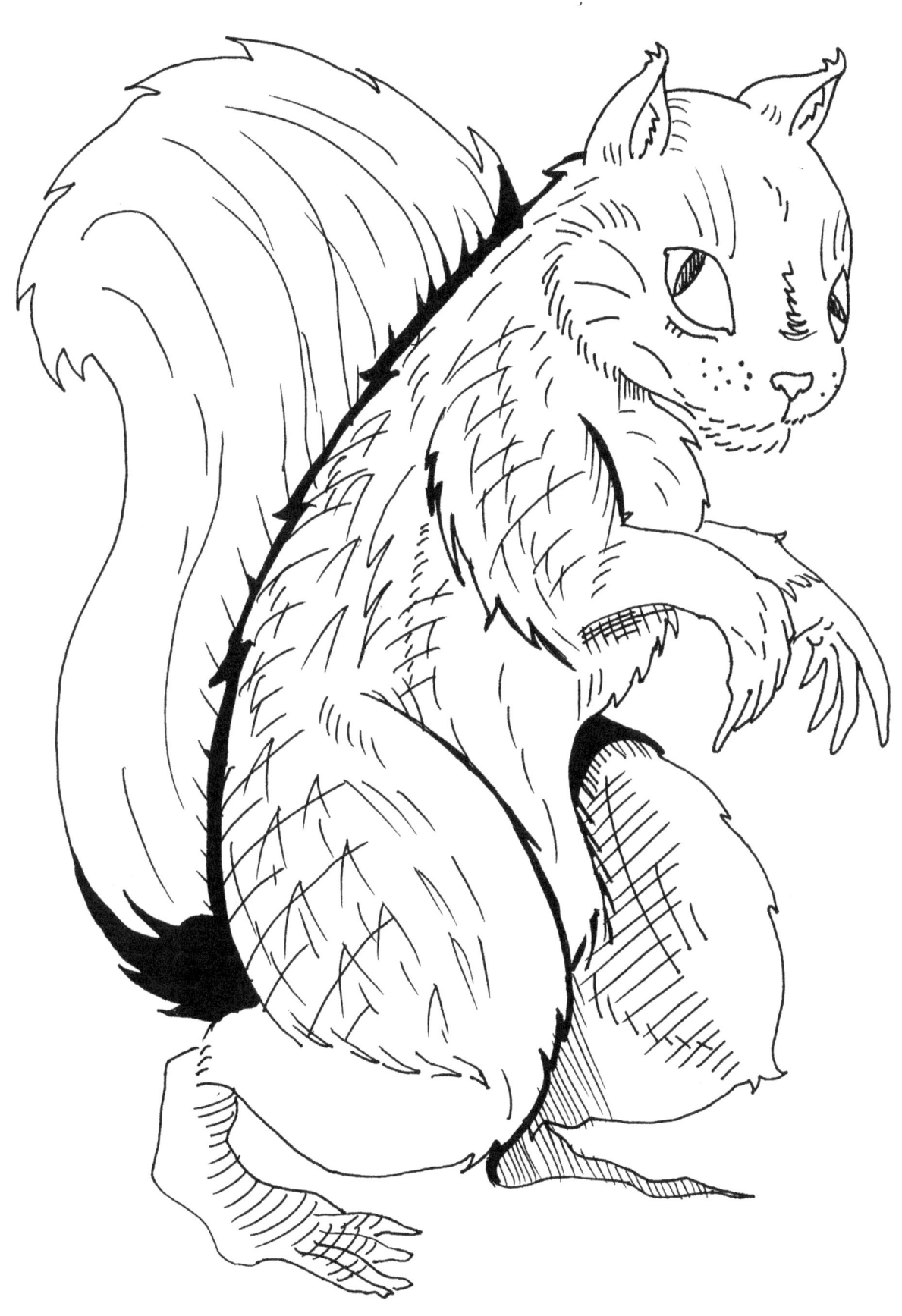

About the Artist

Kyo Smith has been an artist ever since he could hold a pencil or pen in his hand. Art was a welcome escape from the pain of poverty and struggle during his younger years;[Art was] the only thing that anchored him in the face of life's challenges.

Humble and soft-spoken at times, Kyo Smith continues to make his mark on the world... Via ink on paper, one image at a time.

Underground artist until the end.

www.ingramcontent.com/pod-product-compliance
Lightning Source LLC
Chambersburg PA
CBHW082305200526
45168CB00018B/3414